Felt Fantastic

Over 25 brilliant things to make with felt

Sarah Tremelling, projects by Morven Jones

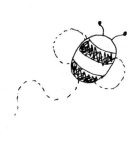

D&C
David and Charles
www.stitchcraftcreate.co.uk

Contents

Introduction

If you already know how wonderful felt is then you can skip straight to the projects – and there are some wonderful ones to choose from! If, however, you've yet to discover the delights of working with felt, then you might want to read on.

Wool felt is made from 100% wool and is the oldest documented textile. It is made by soaking wool in warm water and agitating the fibres so that they 'felt' together. You may have made your own felt in the past, probably accidentally when you put a cashmere jumper in the washing machine and it came out all teeny tiny. Whilst 100% wool felt is the most expensive type of felt you can buy, there are many other cheaper alternatives, including eco-felt (made from recycled bottles), acrylic felt, bamboo felt and wool felt mixes (typically a 70/30 mix of acrylic or rayon and wool).

The main reason I find felt so fantastic is that it doesn't fray. This means that you don't have to faff about with hems and stuff like that. Because it is so easy to work with

it's great for getting children interested in sewing and crafting.

This book is full of projects using felt in many forms. From felt sheets, to felt balls, felt string to moulded felt shapes, you'll find all kinds of different projects here. The book is divided into sections, focusing on felt items for children, for the home, for accessories and for the festive season. Any templates needed are included with the projects and the instructions couldn't be simpler. If you're looking for something to make for Christmas or Halloween, we have projects for that. How about a brooch to jazz up a dull winter coat? If you need something for a child's room we have bunting and mobiles. You could brighten up the dinner table with our floral place settings – the choice is endless.

Whatever you choose, we hope you'll enjoy making and using our projects and taking inspiration from the many ideas in this book. At Blooming Felt we love what we do and hope you will too!

Materials & Techniques

Materials & Equipment

As this book was written in conjunction with our company, Blooming Felt (see *Suppliers*), the majority of the materials used were provided by them, but you don't have to use exactly the same materials. Most of the projects use 100% wool felt sheets. All the felt we use is handmade, which means that it's a lot thicker than commercially produced felt and therefore doesn't need any stiffeners or backing materials. If you plan to use a thinner felt, you will probably need to use a stiffener or backing in order to achieve the same effect as that shown in the book.

We also use lots of embroidery threads in our projects and prefer DMC soft cotton embroidery threads. However, there are lots of different brands available so the choice is up to you.

Some projects use glue to secure different bits and pieces. We use Felt Glue and in some cases Gem-Tac. However, regular PVA glue or Superglue (not for the kids though) could be used and are available at most craft stores.

Buttons and ribbons are available in a whole host of places. Look online for more unusual buttons. You won't need any special equipment to complete the projects. A really sharp pair of scissors, needles and sewing threads and a sharp, large-eyed needle are pretty much all you'll need.

Techniques

There are very few techniques needed to create the projects and those needed are very simple.

Pre-cut shapes and templates

Many of the projects use pre-cut felt shapes, such as flowers and hearts, available from Blooming Felt. These are helpful as they save time. For those projects where specific shapes are needed we've provided templates. Some of these will be the correct size and some will need to be enlarged for larger projects – follow the template instructions.

Stitches

Very simple stitches have been used on some projects, namely blanket stitch and whip stitch. Both of these are very easy to work.

Blanket stitch is a decorative stitch used to accentuate the edge of the fabric. Knot your thread at one end. Insert your needle from the back of the fabric and push it through to the front (number 1 on the diagram). Bring the needle up (2) but don't pull the thread tight. Push the needle back down

through the fabric leaving a loop of thread (3). Put the needle through the thread loop and pull.

Whip stitch is also known as over-stitch and is used to sew or bind fabric edges together. Knot the thread at one end. Push the needle through from the back of the fabric to the front then pass it over the edge of the fabric to the back. Repeat the stitch.

Blanket Stitch

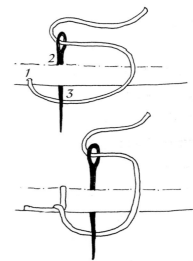

Whip Stitch

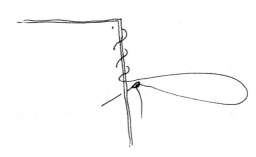

Cute for Kids

Felt Crowns

Dressing up is great fun whether you're four or forty-four. This is a simple design and children will not only enjoy playing with it but also personalizing it with 'jewels'.

YOU WILL NEED

- Two 25cm (10in) squares of felt
- Twenty felt balls
- Three to six wet-felted hearts or pre-cut felt shapes
- Sewing thread

Method

1 Using the *templates* provided, cut out the three crown pieces. Cross stich or glue the sides to the front panel with the cut edge to the cut edge, not overlapping (**Fig 1**).

2 Cut a 2cm (¾in) slit on one end (as shown on the template) and stitch a felt ball on the other side – this will form your fastening.

3 Decorate the front panel with the felt balls and pre-cut felt shapes or the wet-felted hearts. Pin and then stitch them into place. Attach the felt balls to the points, positioning them 0.5cm (¼in) beneath the actual tip, to give extra support and to stop the tips from flopping over (**Fig 2**).

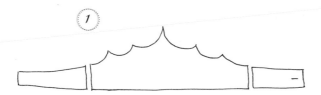

Felt Crown Templates

Shown half size, so enlarge by 200%

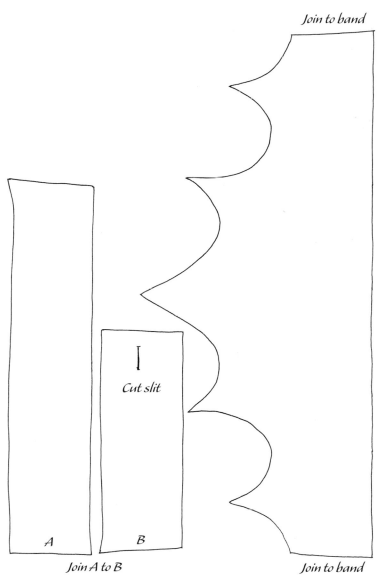

Join to band

A

B

Cut slit

Join A to B

Join to band

Finger Puppets

These finger puppets are, quite literally, child's play! As well as the fun of playing with them, children can get involved in making them too. They are a perfect size to take on a boring car journey or bus ride – just the ticket to pass the time or entertain others. Eight different designs are shown but you could easily create more.

YOU WILL NEED

- A stack of different coloured 15cm (6in) felt squares
- 'Googly' eyes
- Scraps of felt, ribbons and feathers
- Embroidery threads for whiskers and so on
- A few buttons
- Fabric glue

Method

1 The method is the same for each puppet. Begin by cutting out two of the basic *template* shapes provided. Cut out any extra bits such as ears, wings, beaks and so on.

2 Stitch around the curved edge, inserting ears or other features between the two layers, as you go (**Fig 1**). Don't stitch along the bottom edge.

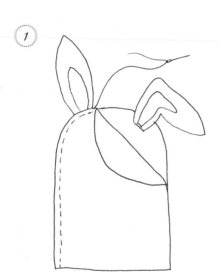

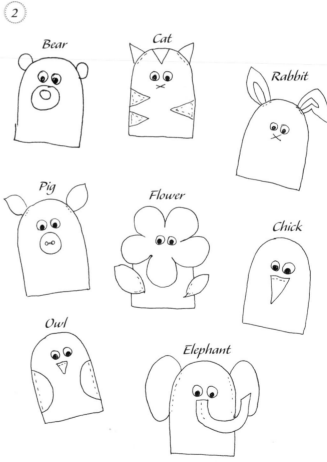

3 Glue on the googly eyes and extra features, such as a button for the pig's nose. Sew a white cross for the rabbit mouth and the bear mouth (**Fig 2**). The designs shown have little in the way of facial features and expressions, which allows the 'puppeteer' to fully use their imagination!

Further Felty Ideas

★ Try creating cute insect puppets, such as bumble bees and ladybirds.

★ A ghost or pumpkin puppet would be great for Halloween.

Finger Puppets Templates

Shown three-quarter size, so enlarge by 133%

Puppet body

Owl wing or elephant ear
Cut 2

Elephant trunk

Owl beak

Owl wing
Cut 2

Chick beak

Flower leaves

Bear ear
Cut 2

Pig ear
Cut 2

Flower

Brown

Rabbit ears

Pink

Pink

Brown

Cat stripe
Cut 4 in black

Cat ear
Cut 2 in orange

Animal Masks

Apart from attaching the elastic, all of these masks can be made with glue, so children can join in. The basic shape is the same for all of the animals – it is the extra bits that make them different characters. So, once you've tried these, you could create designs of your own.

YOU WILL NEED

- Various colours of thick felt, each 25cm (10in) square, as follows:
  owl: mid brown for the main mask, yellow for eyes and rusty red for beak and ears
  pig: light pink for main mask and nostrils, dark pink for ears and snout
  bear: brown for main mask, black for nose tip
  lizard: lime green for main mask, sage green for top of head and pink for tongue
  chick: yellow for main mask and orange for beak and feathers on top of head
  rabbit: light pink for main mask and nose, black for end of nose and ivory for teeth

- Threads to match the felt colours

- Beading elastic 0.5mm wide x 30cm (12in) for each mask

- Medium-weight iron-on interfacing (20cm/8in should be enough for all masks shown)

- Beads and buttons to decorate (optional)

Method

1   Cut a rectangle of felt in the main colour 17cm x 14cm (6¾in x 5½in). Iron on a piece of interfacing the same size as the felt on one side. This will help to stiffen the mask and will also stop it from being itchy.

2 Pin on the main shape template and cut around it. Cut out the eyes (**Fig 1**). Using the extra templates for the animal you have chosen, cut out the remaining shapes.

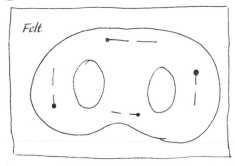

1 *Pinning the template on to the felt*

Felt

3 Using a matching thread, stitch the extra shapes onto the right side of the main mask (**Fig 2**). With matching thread, sew a line of running stitch around the eye holes – this should prevent them from distorting and will give the mask a more finished look.

4 On the back of the mask, stitch each end of the 30cm (12in) length of elastic to each side of the mask, level with the eyes.

Further Felty Ideas

★ Try making a simple bat mask for Halloween.

★ An elephant mask with a long trunk would look amazing made from grey felt.

2

Sewing the ears

Animal Masks Templates
Shown half size, so enlarge by 200%

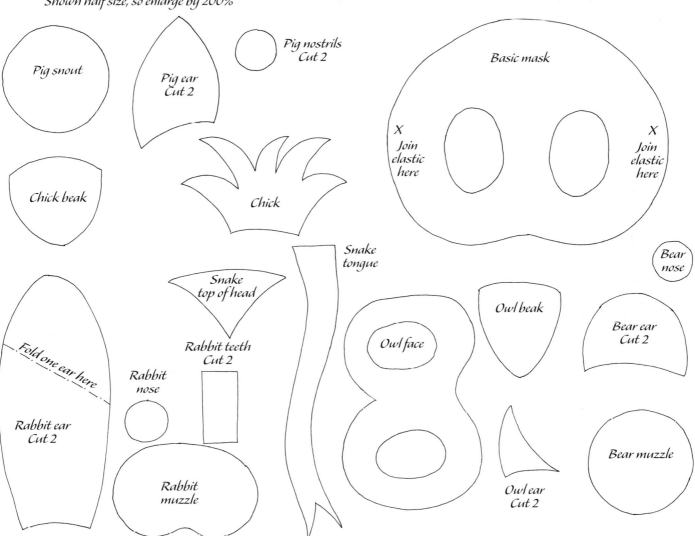

Pig snout

Pig ear
Cut 2

Pig nostrils
Cut 2

Basic mask

Chick beak

Chick

X
Join
elastic
here

X
Join
elastic
here

Bear
nose

Snake
tongue

Snake
top of head

Owl beak

Bear ear
Cut 2

Fold one ear here

Rabbit teeth
Cut 2

Rabbit
nose

Owl face

Rabbit ear
Cut 2

Rabbit
muzzle

Owl ear
Cut 2

Bear muzzle

Flag Bunting

The term 'bunting' originates from a type of fabric made at the beginning of the 17th century. It was generally used to make ribbons and signal flags for the Royal Navy. Today, bunting is thought of as any type of festive decoration, usually fabric, paper or plastic flags on a length of string or ribbon. Our bunting is really easy to create.

YOU WILL NEED

- Felt cord or ribbon 3.5m (3¾yd)
- Seven felt squares each 25cm (10in) square (rainbow of colours)
- Twenty-eight buttons in assorted colours, shapes and sizes
- Twenty-five assorted pre-cut felt shapes (we used a mixture of 9cm/3½in, 6cm/2⅜in and 3cm/1¼in flowers, or cut your own shapes from felt left-over from the flags)
- Fourteen felt balls in assorted colours
- Coloured embroidery thread or fabric glue

Method

1 Using the *template* provided, cut out two triangles from each of the felt squares. Decorate each of the triangles with a selection of the buttons and felt shapes. Glue or stitch these into place.

2 Position the decorated triangles along the ribbon or felt cord with 5cm (2in) spaces between them. Pin the short edge of the triangles onto the ribbon or cord (**Fig 1**).

3 When each flag is evenly spaced along the ribbon or cord, stitch into place with running stitch (**Fig 2A**) or a more elaborate embroidery stitch such as blanket stitch if you want to make a feature of it (**Fig 2B**). Alternatively, use fabric glue.

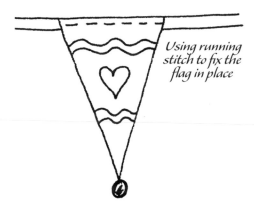

Using running stitch to fix the flag in place

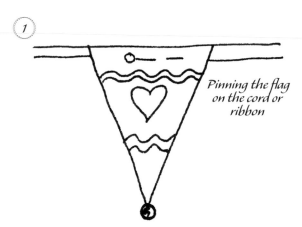

Pinning the flag on the cord or ribbon

Using blanket stitch to fix the flag in place

4 To finish off the bunting, add a felt ball to the point of each triangle. Little bells could be used instead if you prefer.

Flag Bunting Template

Shown three-quarter size, so enlarge by 133%

Further Felty Ideas

★ You could make bunting for a particular occasion, such as Christmas or Halloween (see Halloween bunting project).

★ Make bunting to celebrate a birthday or a Christening by decorating the flags to spell out the name of the person whose event you're celebrating.

Birdy Bell Pull

The traditional bell pull may not be a fixture of the modern home – after all, how many of us need to summon the servants from below stairs? This pretty decoration, however, looks the part at the side of a fireplace or beside a door. By making the shapes double-sided, it can also be hung in a window.

YOU WILL NEED

- Waxed cotton cord 1m/yd
- Two different coloured squares of felt, each about 25cm (10in)
- Tiny amount of yellow felt for beak
- Three sculpted/3D felt hearts
- Eight beaded felt balls
- Four yellow felt balls for feet
- Two felt pebbles
- Selection of pre-cut felt flower shapes (four 3cm/1¼in, four 6cm/2⅜in and two 9cm/3½in) – see *Suppliers* or use the templates provided to make your own
- One bell
- Four 'googly' eyes
- Embroidery thread, about 20cm (8in)
- Sewing thread in your choice of colour

Method

1 Using the *templates* provided, cut out four of each bird shape (two of one colour and two of another), four wings (in contrasting colours) and two beaks (from yellow felt).

2 Cut out the wings and glue or stitch one onto each bird shape (**Fig 1**). Cut out the beaks and glue or stitch one edge to the inside of two of the bird body pieces, i.e., on the opposite side to the wing.

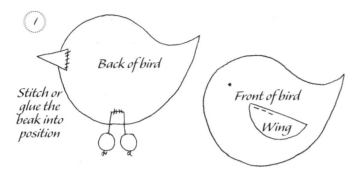

Back of bird

Stitch or glue the beak into position

Front of bird

Wing

1

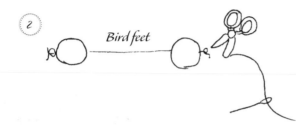

Bird feet

2

3 Make the dangly legs as follows. Cut the embroidery thread into two 10cm (4in) lengths and tie a knot at one end. Thread on two yellow felt balls. Tie a knot in the other end of the thread and slide a felt ball down to each knot (**Fig 2**).

4 Stitch the centre of the thread to the inside base of the bird that has the beak glued to it. Stitch this bird shape to one of the other bird shapes (in a contrasting colour) with blanket stitch or running stitch (**Fig 3**). This will cover the part where the beak has been glued and where the legs have been attached. Do the same for the other bird shapes so that you have two finished birds.

3

5 Templates are provided for flowers if you'd like to cut your own. Alternatively, you can buy pre-cut flowers from our website (see *Suppliers*). Stitch the felt flower shapes to each other, i.e., two 3cm (1¼in) shapes together, two 6cm (2⅜in) shapes together and two 9cm (3½in) shapes together. Stitch a felt ball to each side of the 6cm (2⅜in) flowers and stitch a pebble to each side of the 9cm (3½in) flower.

6 Tie a knot in the end of the metre/yard of waxed cotton cord. Thread the bell onto the cord and down to the knot. Thread your shapes, the remaining felt balls, 3D hearts and birds, onto the cord in whatever combination you fancy, leaving spaces in between. The texture of the felt means they will thread easily and remain in place. Tie a loop at the other end of the waxed cotton cord, for easy hanging.

Birdy Bell Pull Templates
Shown half size, so enlarge by 200%

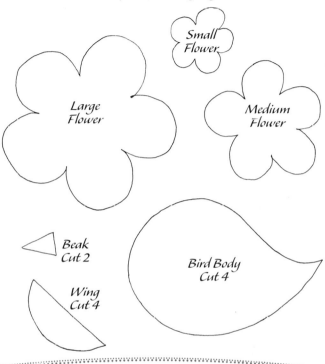

Small Flower

Large Flower

Medium Flower

Beak Cut 2

Wing Cut 4

Bird Body Cut 4

Further Felty Ideas

You can easily vary the themes on the bell pull decoration — here are some suggestions.

★ Use rockets and stars for a boy's room.

★ Use hearts and flowers for a girl's room.

★ Place letters down the cord to spell out a name and make a door sign.

★ Use Christmas or Easter themed shapes to make a festive decoration

Halloween Bunting and Mobile

Every year my children get more and more into Halloween. No longer are just 'trick or treat' bags ok, we have to have more elaborate decorations to scare away (but sometimes delight) ghosts and ghouls! The decorations here use the same templates and similar materials. Three 25cm (10in) squares of felt will make the bunting and the mobile shapes.

YOU WILL NEED

- Black felt 25cm (10in) square
- Orange felt 25cm (10in) square
- White or ivory felt 25cm (10in) square

For the bunting

- Mixture of orange and black felt balls and shapes (ten black balls, nine orange balls, five orange felt pebbles and five orange and yellow swirl felt balls)
- Black felt cord 3m (3¼yd)
- Mixture of black and orange buttons (ten black spotty buttons and ten orange spotty star buttons)
- Seven pairs of 'googly' eyes (fourteen eyes total)
- Black sewing thread or fabric glue

For the mobile

- A polystyrene ring 18cm (7in) diameter
- Orange ribbon 2.5cm (1in) wide x 3m (3¼yd)
- Eight pairs of 'googly' eyes (sixteen eyes total)
- Felt cord (orange or black) 1.5m (1½yd)
- Skein of soft cotton thread (orange, black or white)
- Thirteen orange felt balls
- Fifteen black felt balls
- Thirteen white or ivory felt balls
- Nine black, orange and ivory sculpted felt stars (three of each colour)
- Felt pebbles, two black and two orange
- Glue
- Sharp tapestry needle

Method for the bunting

1 Using the *templates* provided cut out the shapes from the felt sheets – we used four ghosts, six pumpkins and three bats.

2 Take the shapes and decorate the bats and ghosts with googly eyes and the pumpkins with small triangle felt eyes (cut from felt scraps) and a zigzag mouth and stalk (**Fig 1**).

3 Arrange the shapes, felt balls and buttons along the length of felt cord about 10cm (4in) apart. Leave enough cord at each end to make a loop for hanging. Glue or stitch everything into place on the cord (**Fig 2**).

Adding the details

Arranging the shapes with gaps between

Method for the mobile

1 Using the *templates* provided cut out the shapes from the felt sheets – we used four ghosts, four pumpkins and four bats.

2 Glue one end of the ribbon to the polystyrene ring at a 45-degree angle and wind it around the ring, overlapping until the ring is covered. Glue the end into place (**Fig 1**).

4 Cut nine lengths of embroidery thread, each 30cm–40cm (12in–16in) long. Decorate the ghosts, bats and pumpkins as described in step 2 of the bunting instructions. Glue one of each shape into the hanger threads at the top of the ring. Tie a knot in the end of one of the lengths of thread. Thread on a shape, then select five felt balls and a sculpted star and thread these on. Each of the nine strings is decorated differently and you can decide on the final length of each string later. Repeat for all nine lengths. The texture of the felt will hold the shapes in position along the thread (**Fig 3**).

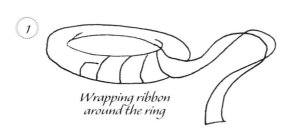

Wrapping ribbon around the ring

3 Divide the felt cord into three equal lengths and tie around the ring, equally spaced. Tie the ends together at the top in a loop for hanging (**Fig 2**).

Making the hanging loop

5 When all of the shapes are on the threads, arrange them in a line, to make attaching them to the ring easier. Thread the end of the embroidery thread onto a strong, sharp tapestry needle and push through from the underside of the ring and out of the top of the ring (**Fig 4A**). If the needle is hard to pull through, grip the point with a pair of pliers. Thread a felt ball onto the thread on the top side of the ring and then go back down again at a slight angle, emerging on the inside of the ring (**Fig 4B**). Tie a knot in the thread up against the ring and trim off excess thread. This should secure the hanging thread in position.

6 To finish the mobile, arrange three threads between each of the black felt cord hanging ties and secure as before.

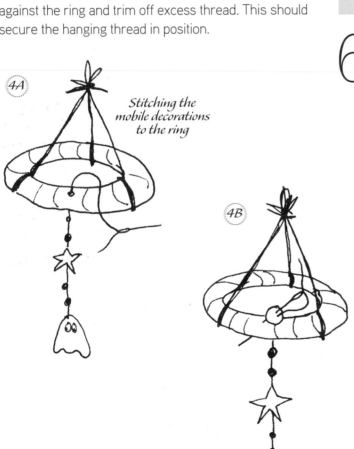

Stitching the mobile decorations to the ring

4A

4B

Further Felty Ideas

★ The bunting and mobile design can be adapted to create Christmas or Easter decorations.

★ Make a jungle-themed mobile with elephants, giraffes, lions and other animlas. Instructions for this mobile are supplied free online at: www.stitchcraftcreate.co.uk/ideas

Halloween Bunting and Mobile Templates

Shown actual size

Bat

Stalk in green

Pumpkin

Features in black

Ghost

Coffee Cosy and Coasters

This colourful set should cheer up your coffee break almost as much as a chocolate biscuit or two, and will keep your coffee hot on the way back from the coffee house!

YOU WILL NEED

For the Coffee Cosy

- One 25cm (10in) square of thick felt
- Thick embroidery thread or 1m (1yd) of bias binding
- Two press studs
- Thick ric-rac braid or ribbon and buttons

For the Coaster

- Forty-nine coloured felt balls, seven of each shade for the rainbow pattern, 1.5cm (5/8in) in diameter
- Strong sewing thread
- Sharp large-eyed needle

Method for the Coasters

1 Arrange the felt balls in a 7in (18cm) square in the pattern you want. Knot a length of thick thread at one end. Using a large-eyed needle, thread a felt ball on to the thread and push it down to the knot. Go back through the hole you came out of and emerge next to the knot (**Fig 1A**).

2 Thread on the other six balls for the first row (**Fig 1B**). On the final ball, go back through the same hole and come out between number 6 and number 7 balls and tie off the thread (**Fig 1C**). Repeat until you have seven rows, each with seven felt balls.

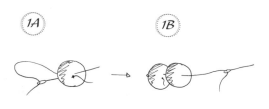

3

Make up the coaster by joining the first balls of each row together as before, then the second, third and so on (**Fig 2**). Be sure to pull the balls tightly against each other as you go along. Finish off by knotting the thread securely in between the last two balls of the rows.

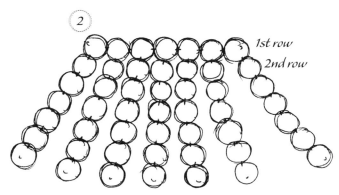

2

1st row

2nd row

Further Felty Ideas

★ Try embroidering your name onto the coffee cosy so that when a jealous friend steals it, it will be easily identifiable!

★ If you're feeling confident after trying the coaster out, why not scale the project up and make place mats?

Flower Place Setting

This table setting couldn't be easier to make and by adding some decorative beads or buttons you can create an unusual set of mats, coasters and napkin rings, which are sure to add fun to any meal.

YOU WILL NEED

For two mats, two coasters and two rings

- Two 25cm (10in) felt squares, in different colours
- DMC soft cotton embroidery thread in the same colours as the felt

Method

1 Using the *templates*, cut out two of each template (one from each colour of felt) and two strips 3cm x 13cm (1¼in x 5in) from the left over pieces (one of each colour) – **Fig 1** shows the layout. Cut out the centres of each of the flowers and put to one side.

Template layout on felt square

2 For the place mats and coasters, swap the centre circles of the flowers so that the orange flowers have yellow centres and vice versa.

3 Using the contrasting embroidery thread, blanket stitch around the edges of the flowers and cross stitch the circles into place (**Fig 2**).

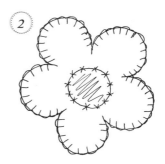

4 For the napkin rings, take a 3cm x 13cm (1¼in x 5in) strip of felt and join the ends together with running stitch or fabric glue (**Fig 3A**). Work blanket stitch around the ends of the ring in a contrasting coloured embroidery thread (**Fig 3B**). The amount of edge stitching is a matter of personal choice – one of the perks of working with felt is the fact that it doesn't fray and so will not need a hem or edging to remain neat. Finally, place the smallest flower over the join and stitch or glue into place (**Fig 3C**).

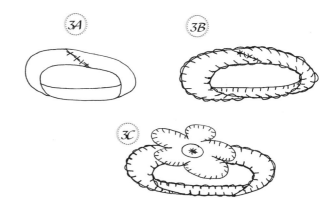

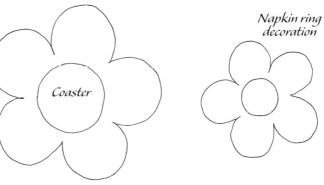

Flower Place Setting Templates

Shown at half size, so enlarge by 200%

Napkin ring decoration

Coaster

Place mat

Further Felty Ideas

★ Why not make heart-shaped place settings in pink or red to use on Valentine's Day?

★ By just using the felt squares as they are, you could easily create an everyday set of place mats and use pre-cut 9cm (3½in) felt shapes as coasters.

Trinket Pot

These little pots make a pretty addition to any dressing table or bathroom shelf – just the place to pop odd earrings. The pot is rather like a cupcake and is cute enough to be a decoration all by itself! The pink/purple pot is described but a rainbow version is also shown. The felt balls were from Blooming Felt and measured about 1.5cm (^{5}/$_8$in) in diameter.

YOU WILL NEED

For the pink/purple pot

- Thirteen dark red/plum-coloured felt balls
- Eleven dark purple felt balls
- Nine lilac felt balls
- Six pink felt balls
- One large woolly pompom or a moulded felt shape
- One 25cm (10in) square of thick felt
- Strong sewing thread

Busy Bee Sewing Set

When I was ten years old my Dad made me a sewing box for my birthday and it is still in regular use. The first thing I made was a needle case and, in doing so, discovered the beauty of felt – it doesn't fray! I later inherited my Great Aunt's sewing box and discovered that she too had made herself a needle case. This needle case and pincushion set pays homage to these sewing memories.

YOU WILL NEED

- Three thick felt squares, each 25cm (10in) square (one each of yellow, ivory and black)
- One black and white spotty button, about 1.75cm (¾in) in diameter
- Six tiny black seed beads (for bee antennae)
- Yellow and brown DMC soft cotton thread
- Black, brown and gold sewing thread
- Small amount of wadding (batting) or stuffing
- Glue suitable for felt or fabric

Method for the Needle Case

1 Cut the case cover from ivory felt 10cm x 15cm (4in x 6in). Cut the inside 'page' from yellow felt 6.5cm x 9.5cm (2½in x 3¾in). Running stitch the page along the centrefold of the cover (see **Fig 1**).

Sewing the 'page' to the inside of the needle case

2 Using the *template*, cut a small beehive shape from yellow felt (for the case front). Decorate the beehive with stem stitch in two strands of brown stranded cotton. Cut a black felt door and glue or stitch into place on the beehive.

3 For the bee, cut two bee shapes from the templates – one in black felt and one in yellow. Cut each shape into four segments and make up two bees using the alternate stripes (**Fig 2**). Glue the edges of each piece of felt together to form stripy bees.

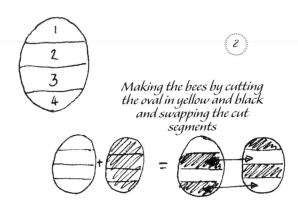

Making the bees by cutting the oval in yellow and black and swapping the cut segments

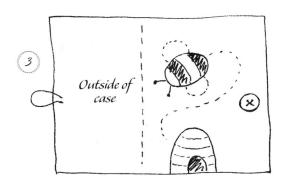

Outside of case

4 Stitch one of the bees and the hive onto the case front cover and embellish with black running stitch from the end of the bee in a wiggly line down the front of the case and into the hive (**Fig 3**). Stitch two of the seed beads to the bee's head for antennae. Using gold thread, stitch two wing shapes. Put the other bee aside to stitch onto the pincushion.

5 Stitch the button onto the front right-hand side of the cover, about halfway down. Make the fastening loop using yellow thread (long enough to go over the button) and stitch to the back cover.

Method for the Pincushion

1 Using the templates provided, cut out two large beehive shapes in yellow felt and one door in black felt.

2 Embellish one of the shapes with stem stitch or running stitch using two strands of brown stranded cotton, stitching lines across the shape. This will be the front of the pincushion. Stitch the black door to the front on the right-hand side.

3 Make a bee, following step 3 of the needle case. You will still have one bee shape left over from the case. Stitch the two bees onto the front panel of the beehive. Add gold wings, antennae and 'buzzy' lines in running stitch and stem stitch as for the case.

4 Pin the back panel of the beehive to the front with wrong sides together (**Fig 4**). Stitch together with running stitch and yellow embroidery thread. Leave a 6cm (2⅜in) gap along the bottom for stuffing (**Fig 5**). Remove pins and insert wadding (batting) or stuffing. Stitch the gap closed.

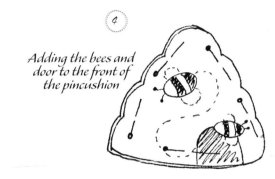

④

Adding the bees and door to the front of the pincushion

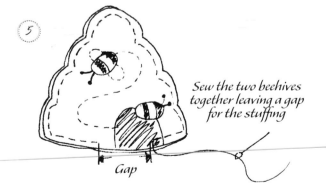

⑤

Sew the two beehives together leaving a gap for the stuffing

Gap

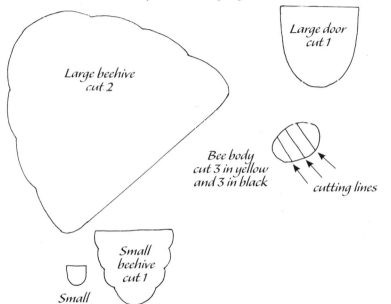

Busy Bee Sewing Set Templates
Shown at half size, so enlarge by 200%

Large beehive cut 2

Large door cut 1

Bee body cut 3 in yellow and 3 in black

cutting lines

Small beehive cut 1

Small door cut 1

Further Felty Ideas

★ Try making a yellow hexagon-shaped needle case with a black page inside.

★ Turn the pincushion into a key fob or bag decoration by adding a ready-made key chain to the top.

Button Pictu[re]

This is a simple, yet striking way to jazz u[p]
can be bought from charity shops and h[...]
overhaul. Our frames measured approxi[...]
pink felt for the heart frame and ivory fe[...]

YOU WILL NEED

- A frame with a flat surface (so the felt frame[...]
  be glued onto it)
- A sheet of felt, large enough to cover the exi[...]
  frame with a 1cm (³/₈in) overlap
- Lots of buttons, between sixty to eighty for
  each frame
- DMC soft cotton thread (red on the spotty fr[...]
  and pink on the heart frame)
- Stiff card large enough to cover the original

Easy Accessories

Brooch Decorations

My Nan always had a little brooch on her coat – it gave her a little twinkle of individuality and always made me smile. These brooches will brighten up any coat or outfit – use them to fasten a scarf or decorate a bag. With the selection of pre-cut shapes, felt balls, buttons and ribbons available from Blooming Felt, you will be spoilt for choice.

YOU WILL NEED

For the cherry brooch

- Two red felt balls
- One green felt ball
- Two colours of green felt
- Kilt or brooch pin
- Short length of string or embroidery thread

For the strawberry brooch

- One dark pink or red sculpted felt heart
- Small amount of green felt
- Small piece of green felt cord or thick string
- Kilt or brooch pin
- Pink and green seed beads

Method for the cherry brooch

1 Cut out three leaves from the green felt (use the *template* provided if necessary). Place one leaf at the back and the other two on top and stitch them together where they overlap (**Fig 1**).

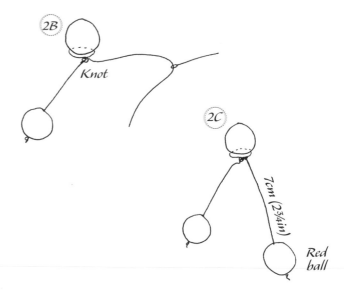

2B

Knot

2C

7cm (2¾in)

Red ball

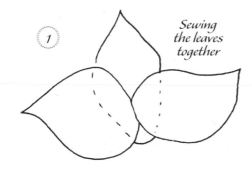

1

Sewing the leaves together

2 Tie a knot in the end of the string. Thread on a red felt ball and pull it down to the knot, using pliers to pull the needle through if necessary (**Fig 2A**). Thread on the green felt ball (near to the base) and leave about 6cm (2⅜in) from the red one. Knot the two ends under the green felt ball (**Fig 2B**). Thread on the remaining red felt ball with a 7cm (2¾in) thread length and knot under it (**Fig 2C**).

2A

6cm (2⅜in)

Green ball

Red ball

3 Stitch the threaded balls onto the leaves at the centre point. Stitch the brooch pin into position on the back of the brooch. Add a few seed beads to the leaves if you fancy a bit of sparkle!

Method for the strawberry brooch

1 From the green felt, cut out the strawberry top using the *template* provided. This may need trimming to size once it's stitched into place as the felt hearts all vary slightly in size.

2 Stitch the green strawberry top into position on the red heart, adding small green beads as you go. Add a stalk of felt cord to the centre.

3 Decorate the strawberry with pink seed beads, widely spaced to look like seeds. Sew the brooch pin across the back to finish.

Brooch Decorations Templates
Shown actual size

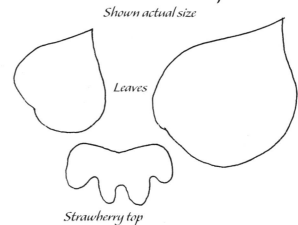

Leaves

Strawberry top

Further Felty Ideas

★ By using the basic leaf template and a mixture of pre-cut felt flowers or hearts and buttons, you can create a variety of pretty brooches to add colour to a drab coat or bag.

Ball and Button Necklace

If you're looking for a pretty necklace to coordinate with a particular outfit, then why not try making this fun necklace using a combination of felt balls and buttons? You could also make a matching bracelet to create a lovely gift set.

YOU WILL NEED

- Waxed cotton cord about 50cm (20in)
- Coordinating coloured ribbon 50cm (20in)
- Mixture of felt balls (four red beaded and four white beaded felt balls were used)
- Mix of coordinating buttons in different sizes (twenty buttons in total)
- Felt star or heart for centre of necklace
- Darning needle

Method

1

Lay out your buttons and felt balls in an even combination that you're happy with, ensuring the felt star or heart is at the centre.

2

Cut a 30cm (12in) length of the waxed cotton cord and using the darning needle, thread the felt balls, buttons and centre star or heart onto the cord, ensuring you leave enough cord at either end to tie a small knot.

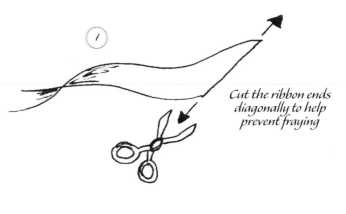

Cut the ribbon ends diagonally to help prevent fraying

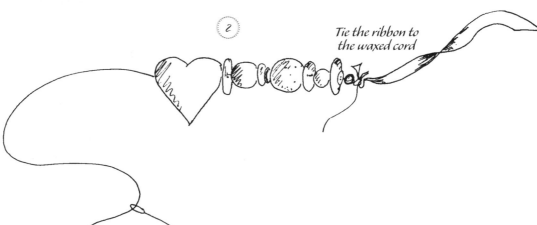

Tie the ribbon to the waxed cord

3 Cut your ribbon in half, cutting it diagonally to help prevent fraying (**Fig 1**). Tie the ribbon to each end of the knotted cotton cord (**Fig 2**). To fasten the finished necklace, simply tie the ribbon in a bow at the back of your neck (**Fig 3**). The necklace can be worn at different lengths by altering the position of the tied bow.

Further Felty Ideas

★ Try threading buttons and felt balls onto a ready-made waxed cord and ribbon necklace, for a multi-stranded effect.

★ For an even easier necklace, simply thread felt balls onto a length of waxed cotton cord and tie the two ends together!

Charm Bracelets

Charm bracelets were originally worn to ward off evil spirits or bad luck and early charms were shells, animal bones and clay. Traditionally, the individual charms signified an important event or person in the wearer's life but today they are more of a fashion item. The charm bracelet bases we used are almost pretty enough to wear alone but the addition of felt balls, buttons and ribbons transforms them into great statement pieces.

YOU WILL NEED

- An elasticated charm bracelet base
- Fifteen to twenty items to decorate the bracelet (two ribbon bows, two sculpted felt hearts, seven buttons, six felt balls, three felt pebbles and two die-cut felt flower shapes)
- A needle and strong thread

Method

1 The charm bracelet base is a concentrated chain around elastic, with the addition of approximately fifteen rings. Begin by arranging your charms in a circle in the order you would like them displayed.

2 Use strong thread to sew buttons onto the felt balls, hearts or flowers. Sew a charm to each ring, looping each one several times for strength. Stretching the bracelet base over a wide tube (a tumbler glass is ideal) makes it easier to locate the rings.

Friendship Gifts

These pretty accessories are simplicity itself. So quick to make, they are ideal as fund raisers for school fairs or Christmas craft markets or to coordinate with outfits or school uniforms. Mounted on pieces of card with a ribbon, they also make lovely friendship gifts – what little girl doesn't need a pretty clip or brooch? Gluing pre-cut, ready-made components together gives a fantastic selection of mix-and-match hair slides, brooches, rings and bag pins.

YOU WILL NEED

- Selection of pre-cut felt flowers
- Selection of buttons, ribbon bows and so on
- Hair grips and slides and brooch fastenings
- Craft glue

Method

1 Gluing is quick, easy and effective but a few stitches will ensure that buttons and so on are securely attached (**Fig 1** and **Fig 2**).

2 Where more than one component is being used, it is best to join these together before attaching them to the slide or brooch fastening (**Fig 3**).

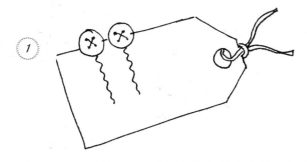

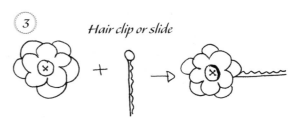

Hair clip or slide

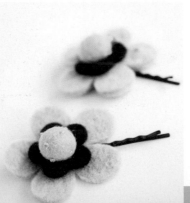

Flower

You'd be hard-pushed
another bag. This cute
also handy to carry ar

YOU WILL NE

- Two squares of felt, eac
  (6in) square
- Fifty-four felt balls (for s
- Waxed cotton cord abou
- Ribbon 0.5m (½yd)
- Pompom trim about 20
- Selection of buttons and
  3cm/1¼in flowers, one
  felt heart, two small flov
- Darning needle
- Embroidery thread

Glasses Case

This is the perfect accessory to protect your sunglasses or spare pair of reading glasses.
The bright and bold design means you won't lose the case easily.

YOU WILL NEED

- Two 25cm (10in) squares of felt in contrasting
  colours (pink and turquoise)
- One felt ball
- Felt string or thick embroidery thread 12cm
  (4¾in) long
- Thick embroidery thread in a contrasting colour
  to the felt
- Sewing thread
- A handful of small seed beads

Festive Fun

8 Join the panels together along the short sides (**Fig 8**). To attach the roof, pin the apex of the gable end to the fold in the roof and at the eaves. Stitch along the edges to hold in place (Fig 9). The house will stand up on its own but for more stability place it over a tissue box or fill it with stuffing. To finish, put a little toy stuffing into the chimney to resemble smoke.

8 *Joining the house pieces*

9 *Pinning the roof in place before sewing*

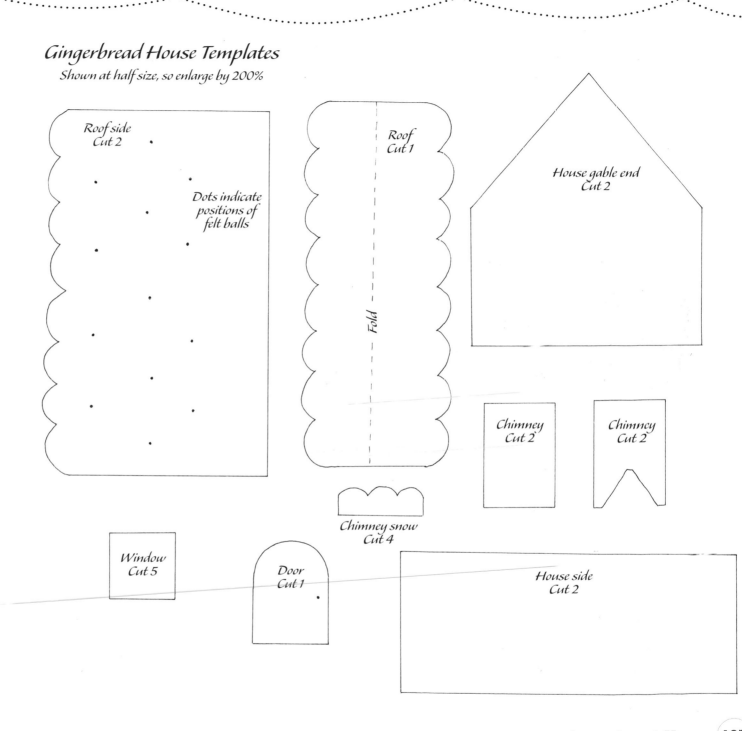

Gingerbread House Templates

Shown at half size, so enlarge by 200%

Roof side
Cut 2

Dots indicate
positions of
felt balls

Roof
Cut 1

Fold

House gable end
Cut 2

Chimney
Cut 2

Chimney
Cut 2

Chimney snow
Cut 4

Window
Cut 5

Door
Cut 1

House side
Cut 2

A DAVID & CHARLES BOOK
© F&W Media International, Ltd 2013

David & Charles is an imprint of F&W Media International, Ltd
Brunel House, Forde Close, Newton Abbot, TQ12 4PU, UK

F&W Media International, Ltd is a subsidiary of F+W Media, Inc
10151 Carver Road, Suite #200, Blue Ash, OH 45242, USA

Designs copyright © Morven Jones 2013 and text © Sarah
Tremelling and Morven Jones 2013
Layout and Photography © F&W Media International, Ltd 2013

First published in the UK and USA in 2013

Sarah Tremelling has asserted her right to be identified as
author of this work in accordance with the Copyright, Designs
and Patents Act, 1988.

The author and publisher have made every effort to ensure
that all the instructions in the book are accurate and safe,
and therefore cannot accept liability for any resulting injury,
damage or loss to persons or property, however it may arise.

A catalogue record for this book is available from the British
Library.

ISBN-13: 978-1-4463-0289-7 Hardback or paperback
ISBN-10: 1-4463-0289-X Hardback or paperback

Printed in China by RR Donnelley for:
F&W Media International, Ltd
Brunel House, Forde Close, Newton Abbot, TQ12 4PU, UK

10 9 8 7 6 5 4 3 2 1

Acquisitions Editor: Sarah Callard
Editor: Jeni Hennah
Assistant Editor: Matthew Hutchings
Project Editor: Lin Clements
Art Editor: Charly Bailey
Photographer: Jack Kirby and Lorna Yabsley
Senior Production Controller: Kelly Smith

F+W Media publishes high quality books on a wide range of
subjects.
For more great book ideas visit: www.stitchcraftcreate.co.uk